Rebecca Livermore

Founder of ProfessionalContentCreation.com

CONTENT REPURPOSING

Made Easy

Create More Content in Less Time and Expand Your Reach

For general information about our products or services, please visit our website at www.professionalcontentcreation.com

Please note that some of the links in this book may be affiliate links, and if you purchase items using the links, I may receive a small commission.

ISBN-13: 978-0692316795
ISBN-10: 0692316795

CONTENTS

Wait! Because you rock!

Have you tried blogging consistently, only to find your blog languishing from lack of consistent blog posts?

I get it. Really.

I used to be a the worst blogger ever. I started and abandoned multiple blogs. I just couldn't get into blogging consistently, regardless of what I tried.

That all changed two years ago, when I discovered the secret to creating content consistently. I now make a comfortable, full-time living blogging.

My Gift to You

As a thank you for purchasing this book, I want to give you my eCourse, The Five Secrets to Developing the Blogging Habit, absolutely free!

To get your complimentary eCourse delivered right to your inbox, go to: http://blogginghabit.getresponsepages.com/

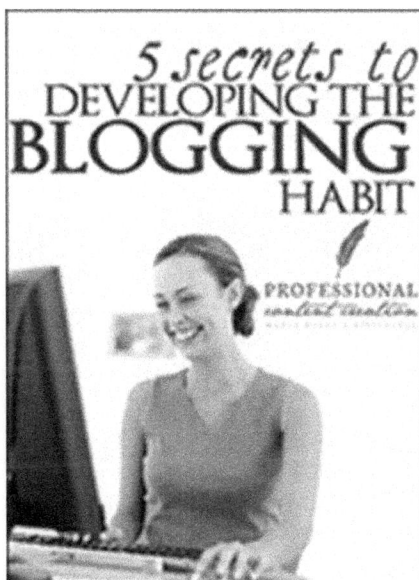

Chapter 1: Why Repurpose Content?

There are tremendous benefits to repurposing content. Before I go into them, I want to simply make the case for content. It has long been said that "Content is king." That term was initially coined by Sumner Redstone. Sumner and his family are the majority owners of companies such as CBS, Viacom, and Paramount pictures, so he knows a few things about content.

What Sumner meant by "Content is king." is that while content distribution channels change, the need for content remains steady.

Considering that Sumner was born in 1923, his prime time was prior to the social media boom that we're all in the middle of, so when he spoke the words, "Content is king," in the mid 90s, he no doubt didn't know then all of the types of content that we have available now.

For instance, he probably didn't know that businesses could market their products and services by "pinning" images on imaginary cork boards. These changes in content media only make his words that much more profound, since distribution channels have indeed not only changed, but increased.

Having such a huge variety of content distribution channels is both a blessing and a curse. It's a blessing because our options are nearly limitless, and it's a curse because our options are nearly limitless.

The problem with nearly limitless options is that having such an abundance of options can be overwhelming. Content repurposing is one of the ways to streamline the content creation process, which helps to reduce overwhelm.

Consider these benefits of repurposing content:

Be Everywhere

A good friend of mine, Pat Flynn, has become known for the concept of "Be Everywhere." While he was first known for his Smart Passive Income blog, he branched out from there to social media sites such as Facebook and Twitter, started a podcast, and built a successful YouTube channel.

As a result of "being everywhere," many people find him on one channel (such as his podcast) that would not have found him any other way.

In addition to the benefit of being found online, on February

25, 2013, Pat discovered another benefit of "being everywhere." His website went down. Now that would be a problem for any of us, but especially considering the amount of traffic and the amount of income that is generated through Pat's site, this was a huge problem. And it wasn't down for just an afternoon or a day, it was down for about a week.

While "being everywhere" didn't replace the approximately $12,000 in income that was lost from his site being down, it did one very important thing — it allowed him to communicate with his fans. For instance, he posted a video on YouTube, explaining what was happening, he then tweeted a link to the video, and also posted updates regarding the situation on Facebook.

While most of us will (hopefully) avoid having our site go down for a long period of time, being everywhere can only benefit our business.

Leverage Time

I'm not going to lie to you; it takes time to repurpose content. Obviously, if I post a blog post, and then do nothing else with it, I don't spend any "extra" time on it. But if I post a blog post and then repurpose it five different ways, I may spend an additional five or even 10 or more hours on it.

But the fact of the matter is, the blog post was a starting

point for me. It already organized my thoughts, had the information written down, and perhaps included data or other information gleaned in research. All of that can be used in the new content I create when repurposing, compared to starting from scratch with having to come up with the concept, doing the research, organizing the main points, etc.

The bottom line is that while it takes time to repurpose content, it take less time to repurpose it than it does to start completely from scratch.

Appeal to People With Different Learning Styles

Some people like to consume content by reading. Others prefer to listen. Still others need visuals. The bottom line is that there are some people who would never read your blog posts, but would listen to your podcast if you have one. Others just aren't able to focus on something in audio format, but will eat it up if the same content is in written form.

Let's consider just a simple way that this challenge can be dealt with through a podcast. A podcast is obviously audio (and in some cases video). An audio version of content won't work at all for a deaf person, and while it may "work" for a person who is not hearing impaired, it may not be the optimal way for ALL "unimpaired" people to learn. Therefore, if the audio from that podcast can be taken and put into written form such as a transcript and show notes, it becomes accessible to a broader range of people.

Target Different Audiences

Related to the learning styles point above, different types of content allows you to target different types of audiences. For instance, you may create a whitepaper that is very scholarly that a lot of people wouldn't read, but they would not only read, but enjoy the information if it was presented in bite-size pieces that are written in a more casual style and posted on a blog.

Repurposing your content can also help you to present the right content to the right people in a very systematic way. For instance, you may post content that is more businesslike on LinkedIn, and content that is more visual and more likely to appeal to women on Pinterest.

You Don't Have to Do it All Yourself

I'll be honest; at this point, I create almost all of my own content. Part of it is that I enjoy it, and the other part is that my budget doesn't permit me to outsource a bunch of my work. However, a big part of my business is assisting other people with the content they create, and repurposing is one of the best ways to do that.

Since repurposed content starts with a base — some type of content that has already been created — the original content has your voice and expertise. It's much easier for a writer or other professional content creator to take your original content and put it in different forms, without losing your voice, than it is for someone such as a ghostwriter to start from scratch.

Getting Started

I hope that by now you can see the benefits of repurposing content. But knowing that it's good to do something and doing it, are two different things. My hope is that through this course I'll not just convince you of the need to repurpose content, but SHOW you how to do it.

If you have any questions along the way, please feel free to email me at rebecca@professionalcontentcreation.com.

I wish you the best in your content creation and repurposing efforts!

Homework

Set up a file on your computer, Google drive, or a paper file where you can keep the content you work on during this course. In the coming modules you'll have spreadsheets, worksheets, etc. to add, and having a place for them will help you keep track of everything.

Chapter 2: Take a Content Inventory

The first step in developing a solid content repurposing plan is to take inventory of the content you already have. You should do this across all of your channels, whether that be your website, YouTube channel, and so on.

Quantitative Analysis

There are two ways to look at the content you already have. First, you can do a quantitative analysis. This is where you focus on the quantity:

- How many blog posts have you already written?

- How many YouTube videos or SlideShare presentations have you created?

- Do you have any podcasts?

- What about content that has been published on other websites? (Be careful with this one — you need to make sure you have the rights to use something that has been published on a site other than your own.)

- What about binders, journals, or other content that has been created, but for whatever reason was never actually published?

- Do you own a book that you can take excerpts from?

Qualitative Analysis

You can also do a qualitative analysis — look at the quality of the content you have.

On a qualitative analysis, you will consider what content may be outdated, or perhaps your perspective on a subject has changed over time.

This doesn't mean that this content is worthless, but it means that it would take more work to repurpose, because you may need to do research to find more current statistics or information, or you may only be able to use the basic idea, and completely start from scratch.

Even if something isn't of the quality that you desire, you can still add it to your spreadsheet (more on that in a minute), if you feel there is any merit in the content at all that is worth salvaging.

I personally recommend doing both a quantitative and a qualitative analysis of your content, because both have merit.

Enter Data on a Spreadsheet

Spreadsheets are generally the best place to enter all of this information. If you don't have Microsoft Excel, you can use a free option such as Open Office, or a Google spreadsheet. (Side note: to meet the needs of everyone in this course, I used Google spreadsheets and docs for this book, so that everyone, regardless of what programs they have, will be able to use them.)

Google spreadsheets can be a bit clunky BUT, I still like to use them because they can be accessed from anywhere. The way I get around the "clunkiness" of Google spreadsheets is that if the spreadsheet I want to create is more complex, I do the actual spreadsheet creation in Excel, where I do all of my tweaking and get it how I want it, and I then upload that spreadsheet to my Google Drive, so I can work on it from any computer.

For this book, I have created all spreadsheets and other documents in Google Drive so that you can easily duplicate them in your own Google account.

Create a Spreadsheet You Will Actually Use

Before deciding what to include on your spreadsheet, keep in mind that a spreadsheet isn't any good if you don't use it, and if you make it too complicated and time consuming to update, you likely won't use it.

On the other hand, a spreadsheet with too little information is little good, and in the long run you'll waste a lot of time by having to go back in and fill out more information later. So just like with Goldilocks and the Three Bears, strive for the amount of information that is "just right."

Here are SOME of the things you'll want to include on your spreadsheet.

*ID — I simply put a number, starting with 1, then 2, etc.

*Title — this would be a blog post title, and if there is no title, you can just put a short descriptive phrase such as, "John Smith interview."

*URL—If your content resides somewhere on the web, put the link to it here.

*Location — this is a great place to list the location of the original source, or in cases where the content isn't online. In this field I may put something such as, desktop computer, and the folder where the content is stored

*Media — text, video, audio, etc.

*Author — this is only necessary if your blog has multiple authors.

ID	Title	URL	Location (if offline)	Media	A
1	Problems with Creating Content	http://professionalcontentcreation.com/pr with-creating-content		Text	RL
2	Business Blogging Blueprint	N/A	Desktop computer, PCC, courses	Text, spreadsheets and videos	RL
3	Small Office Space	http://professionalcontentcreation.com/ho office-small-space		Text	RL
4	Great Places to Create Content	http://professionalcontentcreation.com/gr places-create-content		Text	RL
5	How Following Rules Blocks Creative Content Creation	http://professionalcontentcreation.com/ru blocks-creative-content-creation		Text	RL
6	How to Create a Podcast with Great Sound Quality Inexpensively	http://professionalcontentcreation.com/in podcast-equipment		Text	RL
	How to Blog When You're Not in the Mood to Write	http://www.slideshare.net/ProContentCrea to-blog-when-youre-not-in-the-mood-to-write		Slideshow	RL

Location (if offline)	Media	Author	Quality	Notes	Priority	Status
	Text	RL	Poor	First blog post written, not much to work with	5	Not Started
op uter, s	Text, spreadsheets and videos	RL	Epic	Could easily be made into full-blown course or series of blog posts and other content	2	Not Started
	Text	RL	Poor	Beyond poor. Idea: Starting from scratch, write a blog post on the topic of how to make the most of a small office space	5	Not Started
	Text	RL	Average	Not a ton to work with here, but would make a good SlideShare presentation	4	Not Started
	Text	RL	Average	Not a ton to work with, but could use as inspiration for IB post	3	In Process
	Text	RL	Good	Use to create a SlideShare presentation and a video	1	Done
	Slideshow	RL	Excellent	Use as the base for a blog post on the same topic	1	Done

Example of Content Inventory Spreadsheet. For readability and formatting purposes, spreadsheet has been cut in half. The left half is on top and the right half is on bottom.

*Quality — Not all content is top quality. Some isn't worth repurposing at all, and some is good content, but outdated.

For example, let's say I created a video related to Facebook. Since Facebook makes frequent changes, there is a good chance that a video on the topic of Facebook that I created a year ago would be at least partially if not completely outdated. So I may make a note that the information on cover photos is outdated, but the rest of the content is current.

*Notes — I always love to include a notes field on any spreadsheet, simply because it gives me a place to put information that doesn't neatly fit into any of the other columns. One of the best ways to use the notes feature is to jot down any ideas that come to you for that specific piece of content while you're doing the inventory.

While it's important not to allow yourself to get distracted from completing your inventory by taking a lot of time writing notes, if an idea pops into your head, go ahead and jot it down here. You may also use this column after you've completed your inventory, when you're reviewing it to decide what content you want to repurpose.

*Priority — Since some of your best ideas will be mixed in with your not-so-great ideas, have a column where you can put a priority number. I would use a scale of one to five, with one being reserved for the content that you know for sure you want to use, and perhaps already have some ideas for, and with five being for content that you may not repurpose at all. I would put items that need heavy updating in the five category, since they may not be worth the time it would take to get them up to snuff.

Dealing with Overwhelm

I'll be the first to admit that creating a content inventory can be overwhelming. This is especially true if you've been creating content for a long period of time, and have hundreds or perhaps even thousands of pieces of content.

If that's the case, start with more recent content, such as content that has been created in the last year, or if your volume is very high, in the past six months.

Homework

- Create a copy of the **Content Inventory Spreadsheet** (Note: Use MS Excel or you favorite spreadsheet software) and save it to your in the folder you've created for this book.

- Begin adding the information to the spreadsheet. Do as much of this as you can, but if you don't have time to get too far on it, simply plan to spend a little time each week working on it.

Chapter 3: Set Up a System

A big mistake that I made early on was that I created content without the thought of repurposing it. In the grand scheme of things, that may not be that big of a deal, but it can be helpful to think ahead about how each piece of content you create can be repurposed. Knowing this ahead of time may make it more likely to happen.

What I mean by this is that you can have a set of procedures to follow for each type of content you create. For instance, you may take every blog post, podcast, or webinar and do specific things with that content such as pulling out quotes to use on social media.

Make Repurposing Part of Your Normal Workflow

Content repurposing can just become part of your normal workflow. But one thing to be aware of is that not every piece of content has the same potential for repurposing. For instance, some blog posts will not be meaty enough or significant enough to repurpose.

But just having a list of steps to follow will keep you from having to remember all of the things you may want to do each time, and will make the process easier and more productive.

I created a content repurposing plan for one of my clients for each major type of content that we create. For instance, when she does a webinar, there is a list of everything we'll do to repurpose that content.

In addition to that, I assigned deadlines for getting those things done, and assigned the tasks for them to the appropriate people ahead of time, along with due dates. I put those due dates in our project management system so that they won't be forgotten.

(Note: you can find the sample webinar repurposing plan in Chapter 7: How to Repurpose Webinars.)

Objective for Content Repurposing

It can be a good idea to have an objective for your overall repurposing, or for specific aspects of it. For instance, your whole goal with repurposing your content may be to drive traffic to your site, or may be to grow your email list. Or it may be to be seen everywhere, so that your reputation grows.

When you look at your content repurposing from that

perspective, it will help you to be more intentional and less likely to waste time.

As mentioned above, in chapter 7, you'll find a sample plan for repurposing webinars. Notice the key elements are the what — what types of content are we going to create from the webinar? Note also that the who and when are indicated. Now you may not have a team of people to help you with your content repurposing — and if you don't, that's totally fine.

Note that this document is still a work in progress, and not all bright and shiny. Bright and shiny is all well and good, but don't let perfection keep you from getting your content down on paper (or in a Google Doc as I've done)!

Starting Small or Large

You can't repurpose content until you have some content to repurpose. In some ways that is a no-brainer, but the point is, you have to start somewhere.

You can start small — such as with a blog post, or you can start large, as with a book. Or you can start with something in between such as with a webinar or hour-long podcast.

There are advantages to starting large and there are advantages to starting small. For optimal results, I would recommend using a combination of both processes.

For instance, in Nina Amir's book, *How to Blog a Book,* she writes about writing a book, one blog post at a time. That is a great example of starting small, and ending up with something large.

The great thing about starting small and turning it into something big is that it can make a big project such as writing a book, less overwhelming. It can also give writers an opportunity to test out their material, get feedback, and tweak it before turning it into something big.

But starting big has some advantages as well. For one thing, those who have written a book already have a ton of content they can repurpose. The ideas are already there. The research has already been done. And if you find a person who is capable of helping, you can even hand the large piece of content to someone who can use it to write blog posts, create slideshows, write Facebook posts, and so on.

I'd encourage you to experiment to see what works best for you. However, if you are feeling at all overwhelmed, I would encourage you to start small and go from there.

Editorial Calendars

Regardless of whether you decide to start small or large, or perhaps do a combination of the two, editorial calendars are a great way to plan your content ahead of time. Although it takes a fair amount of time to plan out your content in advance, knowing where you're going helps reduce the writer's block that often comes as a result of having no clue what to write about.

Blogging a book is truly a fantastic way to repurpose content because you'll build your platform while you write your book, so for sure consider adding this option to your content repurposing plan.

Homework

In the folder that you've created to store all of your work related to this book, start a new Google Doc (or Word if you prefer), and answer the following questions:

- What are your objectives for content repurposing? Why are you repurposing content?

    o Do you want to increase traffic to your site?

    o Establish yourself as an authority?

    o Reduce your content marketing budget while increasing your online visibility?

The main thing I want you to do here is to think through your goals, so there are no right or wrong answers!

- What types of content do you want to create?

  o Do you want to create videos?

  o Audios?

Don't worry about what you feel ready for now. Now's the time to dream of what you'll do in the future.

Keep adding to your content inventory.

Chapter 4: Why I Use Google Calendar as My Editorial Calendar of Choice

I've tried a lot of different tools for my editorial calendar, and after a lot of experimentation, I landed on Google calendars for the following reasons:

- I can access the calendar from any computer that has an Internet connection

- I can access the calendar from my phone.

- I can easily share the calendar with team members.

- I can merge, show, or hide different calendars at any time.

- I can have multiple calendars for different purposes inside of one account

- I can color code each entry on the calendar

- I can put a ton of information in the description area

- I can attach images and other items to the each entry

- I can easily move any blog post to a different date if something comes up that alters my schedule

- I can incorporate tasks into my calendar

- And my personal favorite -- Google calendars are free!

A Step-by-Step Guide to Using Google Calendar as Your Editorial Calendar

If I've convinced you that Google calendars are a great way to set up an editorial calendar, follow the steps below, and you'll have an editorial calendar in place in no time.

#1: Create a Separate Google Calendar for Your Editorial Calendar

The first thing you need to do is to create a Google calendar.

To keep things neat and tidy, I like having multiple calendars, for various reasons. For example, I have a separate Google calendar for my blog, Professional Content Creation. If you have more than one blog, or if you write content for other people, you'll likely want multiple calendars, one for each site.

Whether you have one calendar or many is totally up to you, but you'll want at least one editorial calendar, in addition to your personal calendar.

#2: Determine Your Posting Frequency

There are a lot of different opinions on how frequently you should post on your blog. The bottom line is that you need to figure out what will work for you, specifically what you can do consistently. This may be one blog post a week, three per week, or a daily post.

Though not required, you may also want to post certain types of content different days of the week. For example, a written blog post on Monday, a video on Wednesday, and a podcast on Fridays. Deciding this ahead of time will keep you on track when you actually plug the information into your calendar.

In addition to planning out the content on your blog, you'll also want to plan how frequently you'll post on other social media channels. For instance, you may plan to post a video on YouTube once a week, a SlideShare presentation twice a month, and three Facebook posts per day.

#3: Brainstorm a List of Fresh Content Ideas

There's nothing worse than sitting down at your computer, opening your calendar, and having your mind blank out. For this reason, it's best to do some brainstorming and come up with a good solid list of content ideas, before you ever open your calendar. And while this book is focused on content repurposing, since you can only repurpose content that you've created, start by coming up with ideas for fresh content.

Choose one or two of the following ways to come up with ideas:

- Select 5-10 blog categories, and make a list of 5-10 ideas for blog posts under each category.

- Make a list of questions that your clients or customers ask.

- Open a Word document and set a timer for 30 minutes. Write any idea that comes to your mind, as fast as you can. Don't worry about whether or not they are good ideas; you can later delete any that aren't any good.

- If you've set up Google Alerts for your niche, you can skim through the alerts to find ideas.

- If you've jotted down ideas as they've come to you on your phone or in a notebook, pull out those lists to see if there are any content ideas that you'd like to add to your calendar.

The number of ideas that you come up with at a time is up to you. Some people plan a year's worth of content at a time, others only a month. For me, quarterly is a happy medium.

#4: Consider All the Possible Ways You'll Repurpose Content

Remember the content inventory you started in chapter 2? Pull that out and take a look your old content and jot down a list of content you'd like to repurpose.

Especially when you're first starting out, this step may be a bit overwhelming. Because of that, it's best to choose one type of content that you'll initially focus on repurposing. For instance, initially you may want to just repurpose your best blog posts, or perhaps only your podcasts.

Future modules will give you specific tips for how to repurpose different types of content, so for now, if you're unsure how to repurpose blog posts or other content, simply make note of the content you'd like to repurpose "someday."

#5: Plug in Your Information From Your Blog Post Idea List to Google Calendar

Now that you have your list of your blog posts created, know your posting frequency, and have a list of blog post ideas, you're ready to start plugging information into your calendar.

- Start with broad categories. For instance, if you plan to publish a podcast episode once a week, make that a recurring item on your calendar.

- Go from broad to specific. For instance, using the podcast example, replace the generic, "podcast" calendar entry with, "Podcast Interview: Joe Schmoe" or whatever title you're giving to the specific post.

- Keep in mind that these are ideas, not the final post, so don't get hung up on the specific title. For instance, you may write, "Google Calendar as an Editorial Calendar" just to remind yourself of what the post is supposed to be about.

- For the content that you'll repurpose, until you know how you want to repurpose it, you can simply input, something such as, "repurpose xyz blog post." The main idea here is that you're making note of things to keep them from being forgotten. You can flesh them out later!

#6: Take Full Advantage of the Description Box

One of the things I love best about using a Google calendar as an editorial calendar is that I can put everything I need for the blog posts into the calendar entry. Here are some of the things that I put in the description box:

- A basic idea of what I want the content to be about. I use the description box to capture any general thoughts I have about the post so that when I look at it perhaps weeks later, I'll remember what I want to include. Sometimes the title alone is not enough to jar my memory.

- Links to resources – these may be articles that have facts I want to use in the post, or posts (even of my own) that I want to be sure to link to within the blog post.

- Phone numbers, email addresses, or other types of contact information. This is super helpful for things such as interviews, that involve other people.

- An outline of the post.

The image on the next page shows part of what I put in the description box for this post:

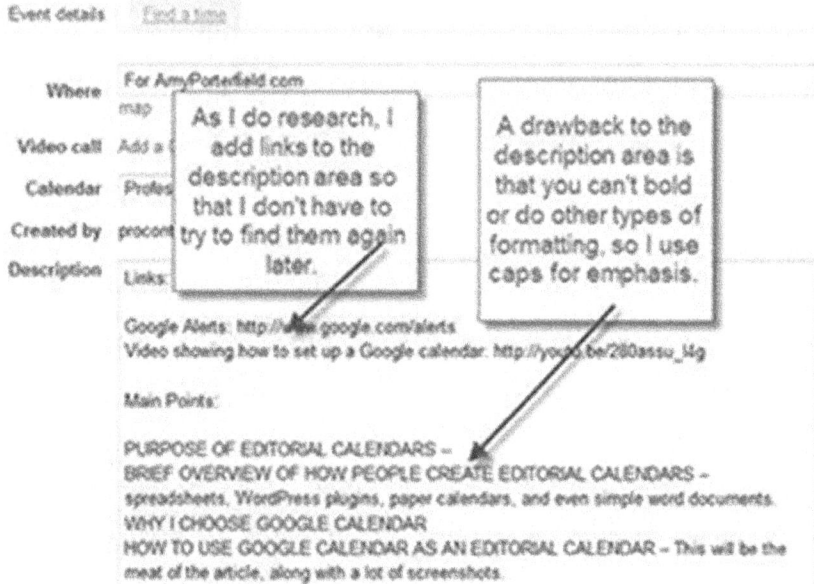

#7: Use the Attachment Option to Upload Images and Other Items Right to the Calendar

In same way the description box helps me keep track of ideas, the attachment option in Google calendar helps me to keep track of things that I want to add to the blog post such as photos.

#8: Add Tasks to Your Calendar

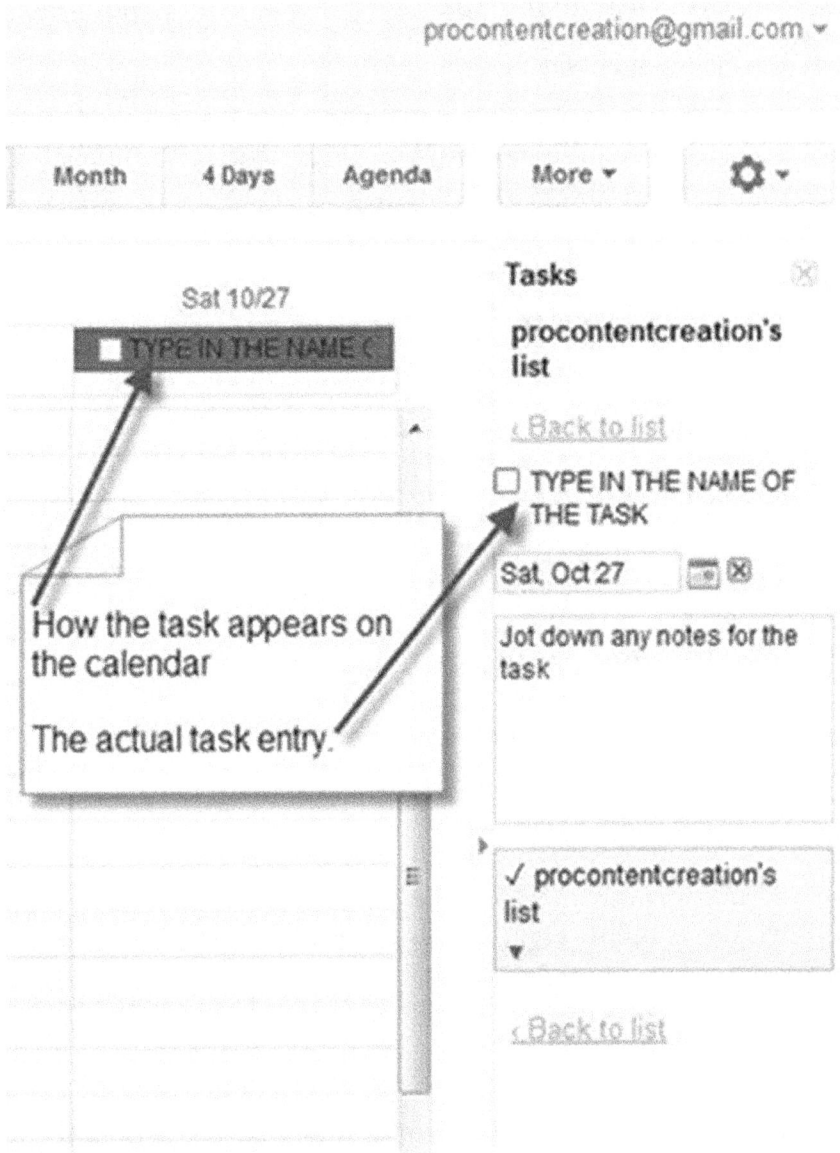

procontentcreation@gmail.com ▾

| Month | 4 Days | Agenda | More ▾ | ☼ ▾ |

Tasks ⊗

Sat 10/27

procontentcreation's list

☐ TYPE IN THE NAME (

‹ Back to list

☐ TYPE IN THE NAME OF THE TASK

Sat, Oct 27

How the task appears on the calendar

The actual task entry.

Jot down any notes for the task

✓ procontentcreation's list
▼

‹ Back to list

A task list is a great way to break into smaller chunks any blog posts that require multiple steps.

Tasks list are especially helpful if you need to do any prep work before writing the post or if you are dependent on anyone else in any way.

For example, if you're planning on interviewing someone for your post, you'll need to make arrangements for the interview ahead of time. In that case, you'd likely want to put the post idea on your calendar, and a task to arrange for the interview on your calendar at least one month earlier than the scheduled post.

You can also use tasks to assign various duties to other team members.

#9: Add Repurposing Plans to the Calendar

Take the ideas you jotted down in step 4 and add those things to your content calendar.

Moving forward, I find this step best to do immediately after I finish the content. I'll admit that the temptation for me is to breathe a sigh of relief once I post or schedule a particular piece of content, and I just want to be done with it.

But my content repurposing works much better — and has a greater chance of actually happening — when I take the time to plan out, schedule and in many cases create my repurposed content before I move on to the next new piece of content I plan to create.

#10: Block out Time to Create Content

Organizing everything on your editorial calendar does no good if you don't actually sit down and create. Regardless of whether you block out time to create content on your editorial calendar, your personal calendar, or your business calendar, schedule time to create. Treat your time to create the same way you'd treat any other important business appointment and only reschedule it when absolutely necessary.

Homework

- Set up a Google calendar to use as your content calendar and begin to implement the steps listed above for filling in the content.

- This is a marathon, not a sprint, so don't expect to get through it all in a day or even a week. In fact, I'd encourage you to spend at least a couple of hours per week working on this until you have a good plan fleshed out for the next few months.

- Keep adding to your content inventory.

Chapter 5: How to Repurpose Blog Posts

My guess is that everyone reading this book has a blog. If not, start one now!

And once you start it, do your best to update your blog consistently. If you struggle with this, I'd recommend that you grab a copy of my free eCourse, *5 Secrets to Developing the Blogging Habit* which you can get at http://www.professionalcontentcreation.com/blogginghabit. That will help you to blog more consistently.

Once you have all that content, what can you do with it?

I'm so glad you asked!

Here are some ways that I've repurposed my blog posts:

Use Them for Newsletters

You can obviously link to your blog posts in emails you send out, but I also recommend using them as content in either broadcast emails, or as part of an autoresponder series. You want to consistently deliver quality content to your email subscribers, and using blog posts is a great way to do so.

I recommend using shorter blog posts for email. This is especially true since so many people read email on their mobile devices, where even a relatively short email can seem long. I also recommend going back to your archives and finding older posts that your email subscribers have likely not seen or else saw, but a long time ago.

Compile Them into an eBook

A compilation of blog posts that you turn into an eBook is a great way to repurpose your blog posts. In my opinion, there are both good and bad ways to do this.

You can use a WordPress plugin such as Anthologize to easily compile your posts into an eBook. The great thing about this is that it's easy. You can drag whatever posts you want into Anthologize and voila! instant eBook.

The problem with this is that you may be tempted to put more into the eBook than ideal and make it cumbersome for readers. So if you use a plugin like this, or even if you copy and paste them manually, be sure to be selective with the content you include.

A better option is to use Nina Amir's way of Blogging a Book.

With Nina's approach, you actually plan out your book and then use your blog to write the book. In her opinion, doing it that way makes for a much better book, and I tend to agree with her.

Use the Information in the Posts for Podcasts

A single blog post may or may not be enough content for a podcast, but a few related posts can make an excellent podcast.

Be sure not to read them verbatim, unless you're specifically creating an audio blog post, as it's hard to sound natural when doing so. What I would recommend is taking the posts and making an outline for your podcast based on the information in the posts. Include enough information in the outline to jar your memory, making sure to include info that would be hard to remember otherwise such as facts and figures or quotes.

Create SlideShare Presentations

SlideShare is a great place to repurpose your blog posts. The way I do it is that I take the main points from the blog post and add them to PowerPoint.

I add in images that complement the information in the post, save it as a PDF, and then upload it to SlideShare. It takes a bit of time, but is worth it!

One great thing about this is that I've taken an older blog post, made a SlideShare presentation out of it, and then used the SlideShare presentation in a brand new blog post. Talk about repurposing!

Use the Post in Social Media

Does your post have multiple points? Take those points and add them to an image, and upload to Pinterest. And of course, link back to the post from Pinterest!

You can take that same image that you created for Pinterest and upload it to Facebook, but keep in mind that tall images work best for Pinterest, and square images work best for Facebook, so it may be best to make two separate images, one for Pinterest and one for Facebook. Even if you decide to use two separate images, you can use many of the same design elements in both versions.

In addition to this, you can also pull quotes for text-only posts for both Facebook and Twitter.

Create a YouTube Video Based on the Post

There are a couple of ways you can turn a blog post into a YouTube video. First, if you made a SlideShare presentation out of the post, simply record an audio to go with it, upload the audio to the PowerPoint presentation and save it as a video.

You can also do a talking head video where you simply talk about the points in the post.

Finally, if the post was related to anything you do online, you could use a tool such as Snagit and make a screencast video.

I hope this gave you some ideas for how to repurpose blog posts, but I'm sure you'll also come up with some great ideas on your own!

Homework

- Keep adding to your content inventory.

- Take five of your blog posts and make a list of how you want to repurpose them. You can use any of the tactics above, or use the same tactic for each of the five blog posts. The main thing is to think about how you want to repurpose them and write it down.

- Repurpose at least one of those five blog posts listed above.

- Add additional repurposing plans to your editorial calendar.

Chapter 6: How to Repurpose Podcasts

Podcasts are a rich form of content to repurpose! This is great news, especially when you consider that they can be a good amount of work to create in the first place.

For the sake of this chapter, when I write about podcasts, I'm referring to audio podcasts. I haven't myself had experience with video podcasts, so don't feel qualified to write about how to repurpose a video podcast. However, many of the things that work for audio will work for video as well, so if you are a video podcaster, use these ideas for audio podcasts to get the wheels turning about how you can apply these or similar ideas to repurposing your video podcast.

Here are just a few ways you can repurpose your podcasts.

Transcripts

Transcripts are such a common add on to podcasts that you may not think of them as repurposed content, but they definitely are! The audio is turned into text. If money is tight, you can transcribe your podcasts yourself, but it's a lot of work, so I recommend hiring someone to do the transcription.

Here are just some ways to use the transcripts:

- Instead of writing show notes, just paste the transcript into the body of the blog post. This works best for very short podcasts, because podcasts that are 30 minutes long are typically a dozen or more pages in length.

- Transcripts can be compiled into eBooks or print books.

- You can pull quotes from transcripts and use them for Facebook status updates, Tweets, and quotes for images that you'll post on Pinterest and other places online.

- Use main points that are between 500 and 1,500 words in length, clean them up and use them as separate blog posts.

PowerPoint Presentations

Podcasts, especially solo podcasts, are in a sense a presentation. Because of that, it works well to take the main points from the podcast and turn them into a PowerPoint or Keynote presentation.

Here are some of the ways you can use the PowerPoint presentation that you created from the material in your podcast:

- If you do public speaking, this can easily become a speech in your arsenal that you can give on a moment's notice. Depending on the complexity of the subject, you may want to add notes to the presentation to jog your memory about key points or facts you didn't include on the actual slides.

- Upload the presentation to SlideShare. SlideShare is one of my favorite places for repurposed content! (You can read more about how to use SlideShare in the chapter dedicated to that.

- Convert the presentation to video (which can be done from within PowerPoint)and upload to YouTube or Vimeo.

Repurpose the Audio

Break the audio down into smaller pieces and use them in different ways. Here are some examples:

- Compile snippets of different podcasts into a new podcast. For example, since I interview a lot of blogging experts for my podcast, I could take the best tip from each expert and combine those tips into a single podcast titled something like, "Expert Blogging Tips."

- Create audio newsletters. If you use AWeber, it has an audio template that you can use to upload an audio to your newsletter, and people can play it from right within the email.

- Use the audio for YouTube videos. One great way to do this is to take the answer to one question, and create a video that answers just that one question. (Or if you have a solo podcast, you can take one point and create a YouTube video from that one point.

These are just some of the many ways that you can repurpose your podcasts, so don't stop with this list. See what else you can come up with on your own!

Homework

- I'm assuming not everyone has a podcast already. If you don't already have a podcast, then simply consider whether or not starting one would be right for you. If you do decide to start one, I'd recommend checking out Cliff Ravenscraft's tutorials. If your budget permits, then I'd highly recommend his Podcasting A-Z course, which you can find here: http://podcastanswerman.com/atoz/. Use the code

PCC to get a discount.

- If you do already have a podcast, make a list of five of your podcasts that you'd like to repurpose, and jot down ideas for how to repurpose them.

- Add those ideas, and ideas for repurposing any other types of content to your editorial calendar.

- Keep adding to your content inventory.

Chapter 7: How to Repurpose Webinars

Webinars are a RICH source of content that you can use other places. My team has transcribed webinars for clients, and it's not unusual for those transcripts to be 30 pages long. Thirty pages is a lot of content to work with!

Now naturally, not all of the content in the webinar is going to be worth repurposing, but much of it will. So any time you do a webinar — assuming you felt the content you delivered was valuable — be sure to have it transcribed, and plan to use as much of it as possible.

I've included a sample webinar repurposing plan at the end of this chapter. Note that this was an actual plan for one of my clients. It is a rough, working document, that we actually use. It's not an exhaustive list of ways that you can repurpose a webinar, but rather ways that made sense for this particular client. So use it as an example, and then also mix in some of these other items below, as well as some of your own ideas.

Here are some ideas for repurposing webinars to get you started:

Transcripts

I've already mentioned transcripts in the podcast module, but wanted to list it here as well. Transcripts are by far the easiest way to repurpose a webinar. You can make the transcript available along with the replay, or just use it yourself in the following ways:

If the content is meaty enough, a single webinar transcript can be turned into an eBook. If you decide to do this, I would recommend interspersing some if not all of the slides from your webinar into the book. Remember that people may want to print the eBook, so I'd avoid adding slides that don't add a lot of value. But in some cases, the images on the slides are a crucial part of the presentation, and in order for it to be well understood, need to be added.

Transcripts from a series of related webinars can be compiled into a more substantial book. Especially if you're going the print book route, it's going to be important to clean up the transcripts and also make sure that everything fits together in a cohesive manner. You may need to add some new content — at least a chapter or two — to make it all flow together well.

Blog Posts

Depending on the length of the webinar and how meaty it was, you can come up with a couple, or many blog posts from one webinar. In the webinar repurposing plan in the bonus section, you'll note that I planned to write two blog posts from the webinar. In reality, I've ended up with as many as six or more blog posts from a single webinar, but at minimum, you should be able to get two.

Quotes for Social Media

Quotes to use on social media. Quotes don't have to be extremely witty, but they do need to be valuable bits of information that are useful on their own.

Quotes can be added to images and uploaded to your various social media platforms, or can be posted without images. I've found that both ways work, and of course, it's less work to post a quote without an image! For best results, do a mix of quotes with and without images.

YouTube Videos

Create YouTube videos using parts of the webinar. In order to do this, you'll need to consider which parts of the webinar would add value on their own. This isn't too hard to do if you have your webinar structured in a way that it's broken down into sections. Each section could be a separate video.

Use them as Bonus Content

Webinars make great bonus content for programs. In that case you don't need to do anything special to repurpose them — you just need to think to add them to the bonus section of a course you've created.

Use them for List Building

You can also use webinar replays to build your list. Make them available free of charge, and have people submit their name and email address in order to receive access.

SlideShare Presentations

What one thing do all webinars have in common? Slides! (Otherwise they would be more appropriately called a teleseminar.)

The great thing about this is that it takes very little effort to upload those slides to SlideShare. I do tend to slightly tweak the slide deck before uploading to SlideShare. For instance, if the webinar was used to promote a certain program that is time sensitive, the final slides, which may be about the program, are of little value later on. Replace those slides with something that is more evergreen, such as, "For more great xyz tips, visit yoursite.com."

One Sheets

Take the main points from the webinar and turn them into a one-sheet or a checklist of actions to take. This can make a great blog post, but it is also great for bonus content in a course, or as a free giveaway to help grow your list.

Podcasts

You can strip the audio from a webinar and use it for a podcast. However, I'm personally not a big fan of this approach because webinars often have visual elements that are an important part of the presentation.

This is especially true if you say things such as, "As you can see in this photo. . ." Hearing something like that would be very frustrating to someone who has the audio, but no visuals, so be sure to keep that in mind as you consider this option.

These are just some of the ways that you can repurpose your webinars. My hunch is that as you begin to develop a repurposing mindset, you'll see more and more ways to repurpose the your webinars.

Sample Webinar Repurposing Plan

This is a sample webinar repurposing plan done for one of my clients. It is "as is," meaning that I didn't pretty it up for this book. Part of the reason for that is that I want to demonstrate that your repurposing plans that are intended for internal use don't need to be pretty – they just need to clearly lay out what you plan to do, who will do the work, and any other details you want to include.

Transcript

- Due 9 days after webinar (provides time for video to be edited, webinar to be transcribed and edited, etc.)

- Person responsible: Rebecca

  o Rebecca will assign the task to a transcriber

  o Rebecca will then proofread and edit as needed and when desired, add to a template.

  o Rebecca will upload the transcript to Dropbox and notify any team members who need to use the transcript for content-related purposes.

  o When applicable, Rebecca will also upload to membership sites.

SlideShare Presentation

- Due 2 weeks after the webinar

- Persons responsible: Client & Rebecca

  o Client to provide individual .jpgs of slides to Rebecca as soon as the webinar slides are completed.

  o Client will also provide a .jpg of a slide that is blank except for things like the header, etc.

  o Rebecca to create a slideshow from the .jpgs that

removes slides that are specific to the program being promoted.

- o Rebecca will also create a slide or two that have a call to action and points people back to ap.com or a specific sales page.

- o Rebecca to upload to SlideShare, write a description for SlideShare, etc.

Blog Posts

- First blog post due 3 weeks after the webinar (taken from first half of webinar)

- Second blog post due 5 weeks after the webinar (taken from second half of webinar)

- Persons responsible: Contract writer and Rebecca

  - o Contract writer will write the first blog post

  - o Rebecca write second blog post

Facebook Posts -- written and added to Facebook Content Plan

- Due 2 weeks after the webinar

- Person responsible -- Social media manager

Cheat Sheet or Checklist (some type of 1-Sheet)

- Due 4 weeks after the webinar

- Person responsible: Rebecca

  - o Rebecca will need some help getting a good looking template created -- maybe one template for a cheat sheet and one for a checklist? I'm thinking a Word doc that I can then use for future ones (saving as a .PDF for distribution).

o Rebecca can work with a designer to have the templates created.

Images with Quotes, suitable for posting on Facebook, Pinning on Pinterest, etc.

- Due 4 weeks after webinar

- Persons responsible: social media manager and graphic designer.

  o Social media manager will provide the quotes to the graphic designer

  o Graphic designer will create images with the provided quotes

  o Social media manager will add the image quotes to the editorial calendar and post to the various social media platforms according to the plan.

Some type of audio/video content

- This fits into the "someday" category. I (Rebecca) will need to experiment with things like audio and video editing. I'm just adding it to this document because I want it to stay on our radar as a possible type of content to do someday. I will also want to do this with our podcasts.

- Any other bright ideas we come up with! (Feel free to add to this document!)

Notice that what is written above is vague. While it helps to be specific in a plan, it's important to get ideas down and include them on the plan even if they aren't totally fleshed out yet. This keeps those things from being forgotten.

Homework

- If you're not already doing webinars, consider adding webinars to your marketing mix.

- If you are doing webinars, check out the sample webinar repurposing plan above, and adapt it for your own use.

- Continue adding to your content inventory and your content calendar

Chapter 8: How to Repurpose Content for SlideShare

SlideShare is by far one of my favorite ways to repurpose content. I've put repurposed content on SlideShare created from podcasts to webinars to blog posts to eCourses. In some cases, such as a webinar or live presentation, you may already have a slide show created, and uploading it to SlideShare is an easy thing to do.

While you can upload a presentation as is, without making any changes, presentations that are optimized for SlideShare tend to do better.

For instance, in a live presentation, you may use photos without any, or very few words. That works fine, since you, the speaker, is, well, speaking.

But without your words, slides that are photos alone, have very little impact, even if they are entertaining to view. You can actually add audio to a SlideShare presentation, so if your presentation was recorded, then by all means, feel free to leave it as is, without text, and just upload the audio so it all makes sense to the people who view it on SlideShare.

Now here are a few tips for optimizing SlideShare presentations:

Add Audio

As I already mentioned above, the good news is, you can add audio to SlideShare presentations. The bad news is, it takes a bit of work to sync the audio to the right slides, but it is definitely doable.

In addition to potentially making the presentation more enjoyable, audio also makes a presentation stand out, due to the audio symbol, and the words, "Slidecast Audio Track Inside" displayed in the upper left corner.

Add Video

You can upload a YouTube video alone to SlideShare, and you can also add a video in at any other point in the presentation. This is a great way to add some extra punch to a standard slideshow, and as with the Slidecasts, there is a visual cue that there is "something extra" in the presentation.

Use Words Wisely

A common no-no in standard presentations is using too much text. But as I've alluded to above, unless you use audio or video in your SlideShare presentations, they are pretty meaningless without words.

While words are important, it's important to make sure the words are easy to read. I've seen some presentations where there is so much text on the slides, the print is tiny, and I either can't — or won't — read it because it's just difficult to do so.

Tell Stories

I love using a storytelling format in my SlideShare presentations because they keep people clicking from one slide to the next, all the way through the end.

Include Links

SlideShare can be a good source of traffic to your website or things you're promoting such as affiliate products, so be sure to include links where it makes sense to do so.

Use links in the same way you would on a blog — in places where it makes sense to include them. For instance, if your presentation is about green widgets, and you use the word, "green widgets" various places in the presentation, it makes sense to occasionally hyperlink the words to your site where you sell green widgets.

You can also add links to the images so that when people click on the images, they go to a site of your choosing. You can even add words such as, "click here," with an arrow to your last slide, to encourage people to click through.

Call to Action

End with a call to action. Always include a call to action in your last slide. "Click here," "read more about 'x,'" etc.

Update Your SlideShare Presentations

If you choose to use a slide presentation that was originally from a live webinar or a live presentation, be sure to remove any slides that don't make sense outside of the live presentation.

For instance, if the webinar was used to promote a program that was only available for a limited time, remove the slides that refer to the program. If desired, you can replace them with slides with a different call to action.

This can also be done any time information has changed that results in a presentation having outdated information.

For instance, if you have a presentation that is mostly current, but has some outdated statistics, you can make those changes on your PowerPoint presentation that you have saved on your computer, and replace the old SlideShare presentation with the one with the updated information.

Being able to replace a presentation with an edited presentation without losing any of the social proof is one of my favorite things about SlideShare.

The bottom line is that you can repurpose almost any type of content on SlideShare.

Homework

- If you don't already have a free SlideShare account, open one.

- Check out some of the top SlideShare presentations for inspiration.

- Take one of your blog posts or other pieces of content and create a PowerPoint presentation from it and upload it to SlideShare. Note: If you do not have PowerPoint or Keynote, use the free presentation program on Google Drive.

- Continue adding to your content inventory and your content calendar.

Chapter 9: How to Outsource Content Repurposing

One of the things I love most about content repurposing is that more than any other type of content creation, content repurposing is something that is more easily outsourced.

The reason that you can more easily outsource content repurposing is because the person who will be doing the repurposing has a good solid foundation to start with. That foundation is filled with your knowledge, expertise, and even your voice — your own unique way of seeing the world and expressing your thoughts about it.

Because of this, you can repurpose content and have it still sound like you — and unless the person you outsource to drastically changes your message, you don't have to worry about the content they put out on your behalf contradicting anything you believe or teach.

Since I'm a content creator myself, I don't hire a lot of people to create content for me — but I do hire people to repurpose my content, because it enables me to crank out more content than I could on my own, and yet since I had a hand in it, I feel good about my name being on the content.

How I Outsource Turning Blog Posts into PowerPoint Presentations

There are many ways you can outsource content repurposing, but the primary content repurposing that I outsource is turning my blog posts into PowerPoint presentations and videos.

Here are the specific steps I take:

1. I find the piece of content that I want to have repurposed such as a blog post.
2. Open a Google Document, and insert a table with three columns.
   The three columns are slide #, text to go on the slide, and notes/instructions. I then go through the blog post and decide what I want to go on each slide.
3. I then give that document to one who specializes in PowerPoint and have her get started on it. About a third of the way into it, she sends me what she's done so far, and I give her feedback and then she completes it.

4. I have her create two versions of most presentations. The second version is identical to the first version except that it also includes animations. I upload the one without animations to SlideShare, and add an audio track to the one with animations, save it as a video, and then upload that to YouTube.

As you can see from what I've written above, even with help, this is still a lot of work for me, and yet outsourcing parts of it saves me a lot of time.

To give you an idea of how this all works, here's an example of one I actually did, step by step.

1. I selected a blog post I'd already written. Here is an image of an original blog post on the topic of how to create a podcast with good sound quality inexpensively.

How to Produce a Podcast with Great Sound Quality Inexpensively

by Rebecca Livermore on in Content Creation, Podcasting

I received the following email from one of my podcast listeners:

> Hi Rebecca
>
> Thanks for a great podcast. You have really wonderful audio quality for your interviews. Are you interviewing over Skype? If

2. I planned out the content for the slideshow and YouTube video. Below is a screenshot of a Google Doc that I've given to the outsourcer.

This is a 'script' for a PowerPoint Presentation

This is for use on both SlideShare and YouTube. So animations will be nice for when I convert it into a video for YouTube, but bear in mind that there are no animations on SlideShare.

Please don't hesitate to let me know if you'd like to connect via Skype as well.

Slide #	Text to go on slide	Notes
1	How to Create a Podcast With Great Sound Quality Without Breaking the Bank	**This is the title slide. It's the most important slide from a graphics perspective. It really needs to be visually appealing to stand out on SlideShare and YouTube**
2	Brought to you by Rebecca Livermore, and ProfessionalContentCreation.com	Link the website URL with the following link http://www.professionalcontentcreation.com/?utm_source=ss&utm_medium=social&utm_campaign=blog Also please incorporate my logo into the design of this slide. And hyperlink the image to go to my main website as well https://docs.google.com/file/d/0B-ekgX8HeHKpWFo0eFpMcUxqeEU/edit?usp=sharing

3. I assigned the task to the outsourcer. Here is an image of the Slideshow she created:

4. Record an audio of me teaching the content in the slide presentation. Upload it to the PowerPoint presentation that has the animations, save it as a video, and upload it to YouTube.

As you can see, I'm still heavily involved in the process when I outsource, but it still saves me a lot of time. Also, since I pay the people who help me a respectable amount but an amount that is less than what my own time is worth, this is actually a way to increase my income as well.

Tips for Successful Outsourcing

Outsourcing is like anything — sometimes the results are good and other times, not so much. Here are some tips to make the process go more smoothly:

1. Don't expect any one person to be talented in everything.

With any luck, you may be able to find a content manager who can handle a wide variety of your content, including certain types of content repurposing. But it's highly unlikely that you'll be able to find someone who is a great writer, videographer, audio technician, and graphic designer.

Instead, what I would look for is a good content manager who understands the big picture of what needs to be done and has good organizational and project management skills. Allow that person to operate in areas of strength such as writing or video production or social media, and then task them with overseeing other aspects of content repurposing.

2. Express your expectations clearly.

For example, if you want the person to use a lot of images, let them know that and also give them specific instructions about the type of images you're looking for, where they can find the images (along with your login credentials for the stock image site you use), and so on.

3. Give them feedback about the work they do.

Even if you've given people very specific instructions and set expectations, that doesn't mean they'll get it right the first time. Or the first three or five times. But unless the person isn't a good fit for you, with feedback, they should be able to adapt to your style so long as you let them know what you do and don't like. Be sure to do so in a positive and encouraging manner.

4. Have realistic expectations regarding how long content repurposing takes.

Obviously, someone you hire shouldn't have to spend several hours on creating a single image for Pinterest, but images and other types of content can take a good amount of time to create, so don't expect someone who works part time to produce massive amounts of content.

5. Measure the results.

Regardless of whether you create all of your content yourself or pay someone to help, it is important to know the impact of the content that you create. The best way to do so is to track the amount of traffic to and from different sites. For instance, you can see how much traffic comes to your website through various channels such as SlideShare, Pinterest and YouTube.

If you want more specific information, it's best to create tracking links using this tool.

You can also track how many views, shares, likes, comments and so on that the different pieces of content receives.

Sharing Files

If you outsource some of your content repurposing, or if you have any team members whatsoever, chances are, you'll need to share files with them.

Here are some of my favorite tools for file sharing:

Google Drive: Google Drive is my primary way to share files with team members. I got 100 free gigabytes of storage when I purchased my Google Chromebook, and since I was already using Google Drive, it just made sense to up my usage of it when I got all of that free storage.

I store all of my documents and other files that I want to share with team members on Google Drive. This is everything from audio files that I share with transcribers to "Word" documents, to slide presentations to images.

One thing that I love about Google Drive compared to some of the other file sharing options is the ease of collaboration. Multiple people can edit a document, even at the same time, without a problem.

This can't be done with other options such as Dropbox. Having said that, Dropbox is also a great option!

Dropbox: Dropox is great for sharing files, particularly larger files that can't be emailed, such as videos. Since I use Google Drive so much, I don't use Dropbox as much, however many of my clients use Dropbox and therefore, by default, I do as well. The advantage to Dropbox over Google Drive is that the documents you upload to Dropbox tend to be the "real" versions of Excel or Word, if that is what you use.

While I like Google Docs, it is more clunky than the Microsoft equivalent. On the other hand, documents in Dropbox cannot be edited at the same time, and if multiple people work on things, you may end up with several different versions of the same document. Because of this, I would say that Dropbox is great for sharing files and Google Drive is good for both sharing AND collaboration.

YouTube: I use YouTube to share tutorial videos with my team members. This can be done simply by recording the video and then uploading it to YouTube and making it private or unlisted. Private videos can only be viewed by the specific people you give access to, while unlisted videos can be viewed by anyone with the link — but they don't show up in searches. Obviously, if information in the videos is very sensitive, you will want to make the video private rather than just unlisted.

Getting Started with Outsourcing

I personally recommend taking baby steps when it comes to outsourcing any of your work, including content repurposing. The reason for this is that outsourcing is a skill, just like any other skill. If you've never outsourced anything, it can be tough to know how to delegate.

In addition to this, it takes time to train someone, and if you have several people to train all at once, or if you hire a fulltime person such as a VA right off, it may be hard to take the time to prepare work for the person.

What I've done up to this point is hired people for very specific tasks. For instance, I have one contractor who helps me with PowerPoint creation, and another one that helps me with audio and video editing, and a few contractors that help me with client writing projects. Soon enough I will hire a full time VA or project manager.

Where to Find Contractors

Contractors can be found numerous places. I've had both good and bad luck with oDesk and eLance. The great thing about these options is that you can get work done without an ongoing monthly commitment.

You can also test people out on small projects before making a commitment. If you use one of these services, I would recommend taking the time to read the reviews and avoid going with the cheapest person. Cheaper isn't always better!

For one off projects, Fiverr. There is a lot of crappy work done through Fiverr, but there is also a lot of good quality work, and the worst case scenario is that if a job was done poorly, you're only out $5.

I've also hired contractors via word of mouth recommendations, as well as put some talented family members to work.

If you want some help with finding contractors and don't want to have to weed through the possibilities yourself, agencies are a good way to go. For VAs in the Philippines, the most highly recommended person is Chris Ducker, and his firm, Virtual Staff Finder. A good, U.S. based company is eaHELP. I will likely go with an agency such as this when I'm more ready for substantial, ongoing work.

The bottom line is that it just doesn't pay to do it all yourself, so at the very least, dip your toe into the content repurposing outsourcing stream in order to get more content out there to maximize your content marketing efforts.

Homework

- Set a timer for 15 minutes and jot down everything you can think of that you can potentially outsource (even the ones that seem like dumb ideas)

- If you're brand new to outsourcing, pick just one of those ideas to start with. When you're first starting out, it's best if this is something simple like a project (e.g. creation of a PowerPoint presentation) rather than a long-term commitment.

- Head to oDesk and find someone to hire for that one project. Remember to read reviews first, and start with something small. If you're unhappy with the first person you select, try another contractor.

- If you're ready for more permanent help, check out an agency such as Virtual Staff Finder, eaHELP, or HireMyMom

- Continue adding to your content inventory and content calendar. (You might even want to hire a VA to help you with this!)

Conclusion

I hope that through the pages of this book that you've found not only some inspiration but ample tips to get you started on your content repurposing journey.

The task may seem overwhelming, and it certainly won't get done overnight. In fact, expect it to be a long process that in some ways, never ends.

To keep that from discouraging you, keep records of your accomplishments. For example, you may want to keep a record of the number of original pieces of content that you've created, and the number of pieces of content that you've repurposed from that content.

You'll likely find it helpful and encouraging to check your stats in Google Analytics so that you'll be able to see the impact that your repurposed content has made on your overall traffic, and at least potentially on your bottom line in terms of your income.

Thank you!

I hope you enjoyed this book, *Content Repurposing Made Easy* and that you feel motivated and equipped to make a difference with your content.

With the URL"s below, you'll be able to rate this book, tweet about it, and share it on Facebook. Please take a moment to do that, as I'd be incredibly grateful for your help in spreading the word to other content producers who need help in their content journey.

I'd also appreciate it if you'd leave a short review on Amazon. That will help me improve not only this book, but other books as well, and it will also help others to discover *Content Repurposing Made Easy.*

Thanks so much! I wish you great success on your journey.

Rebecca Livermore
http://professionalcontentcreation.com/

Visit my Amazon Author's Page. Go to
http://www.amazon.com/. Search for Rebecca-Livermore and select my author's page.

Follow us on Facebook and Twitter!

Twitter --https://twitter.com/rlivermore (@rlivermore)

Facebook -- https://www.facebook.com/ContentCreation

Do you struggle to blog consistently?

Grab my free eCourse, *5 Secrets to Developing the Blogging Habit*

http://blogginghabit.getresponsepages.com/

About the Author

Rebecca Livermore has been a freelance writer since 1993. She got her start writing for print magazines, and then transitioned into writing for the web in 2006. Now she prefers to write for the web, but still writes for print magazines on occasion.

In addition to writing on her own website, she is a staff writer for *iBlog Magazine* and also does some private client work as well. Her impressive client list includes top experts in the blogging, social media, and content marketing industries including but not limited to:

*Amy Porterfield
*Michael Hyatt
*Pat Flynn
*Marcus Sheridan
*Chris Ducker
*Social Media Examiner
*. . . and more

If you need blog writing services, Rebecca has a small number of slots available for her "Blogging Your Voice" service. On a very limited basis, Rebecca takes on private consulting clients. You can check her current availability here: http://professionalcontentcreation.com/coaching.